Organising Idea No. 4

A monograph published for the
EUROPEAN THERAPY STUDIES INSTITUTE

The APET model

Human Givens Publishing Ltd
for the European Therapy Studies Institute
Chalvington, East Sussex BN27 3TD, United Kingdom

Printed in Great Britain

ISBN 1 899398 06 6

The APET model

**How new discoveries about the
pattern matching properties of
the brain can lead to more effective
counselling and psychotherapy**

Joseph Griffin & Ivan Tyrrell

"It seems that the human mind has first to construct forms independently before we can find them in things."

Albert Einstein

"Use the light that is within you to regain your natural clearness of sight."

Lao-tzu

Organising Ideas

"All scientific knowledge is a correlation of *what* is seen
with the *way* that it is seen."

Henri Bortoft, *The Wholeness of Nature*

In all fields confusion flourishes, mistakes are made and harm is done when we forget that the *way* we look at phenomena is dependent on an active effort of imagination and thinking. We are not mechanical recording instruments looking out on a fixed world (although this is certainly the philosophy of science which is usually communicated by the way science is taught in schools, presented in popular books and revealed in television programmes). We *organise* what we see through what we believe we know.

When a field of study is confused about something, it usually needs a new organising idea.

An organising idea plays an active role in shaping our perception, thinking and research and is always larger than earlier ideas because it has to explain the anomalies that previously caused confusion.

This paper, one of a series commissioned by the European Therapy Studies Institute, offers a new organising idea.

ETSI 2001

"All things ... linked are,
That thou canst not stir a flower,
Without troubling of a star."

Francis Thompson

The APET model

HOW DOES a virtuoso violinist perform the immense complexities of a concerto – the ethereal harmonies, melodies, tones, changing rhythms and moods – and thereby entrance an audience? How do we recognise an old friend we haven't seen for twenty years? Why are there not millions more car crashes every day as motorised populations around the world negotiate complex urban road systems at speed? How does a farmer know exactly the right moment to begin harvesting? Why do placebos help people? What happens in our minds when we start to laugh *before* something funny happens? In what subtle way does a craftsman know when his work of fine art is complete? How do we pick up what someone else is feeling? And why do we sometimes feel anxious without a conscious reason for it?

The answer to all of these questions is to be found in a new understanding of how our brains function as profoundly complex, metaphorical pattern-matching organs. Pattern matching not only explains all the small miracles of everyday living, it is the key to understanding mental health and reversing many mental disorders.

Pattern matching explained

By the time we are born, nature has provided us with templates for certain instinctive behaviours, programmed into us during our REM sleep in the womb.[1] Newborns know immediately how to begin developing rapport with the adults on whom they depend for food, warmth, safety and comfort. They know instinctively to draw noisy attention to themselves to make sure they are fed and comforted. These templates, that help us survive, grow and fulfil our fundamental emotional needs, are the human givens – internal patterns for which we seek fulfilment in the environment. They are, however, necessarily incomplete. This is because the world is not a uniform, predictable place and all creatures need to be able to respond in a flexible way in order to survive in it. So the myriad templates laid down in the baby say, in effect, "Look in your environment for something *like* this to complete the pattern". That is why a baby can happily suckle on any shape or size of nipple, a rubber teat, or even a finger for a while. We call these incomplete patterns 'metaphors'.

This metaphorical pattern-matching process, giving living things flexibility to adapt, is something we share with all life forms. A bird, for example, has a nest-building metaphorical template that says, in effect, "Look for twig-like things to build the nest with and soft, feathery material to line the nest with". So the bird is able to use a variety of materials – straws, wire, paper, plastic foam, cloth scraps etc. – to construct its nest.[2]

The more complex the life form, the more varied and rich are the instinctive templates laid down in the creature. No animals we know of are more adaptable than human beings who clearly have the greatest amount of flexibility of any species on the planet. We can, therefore, conclude that the pattern-matching programming that exists in humans has a capacity for a much larger environmental input than one finds in other species.

A baby's communication skills are a simple illustration of this. Scientists have developed many ingenious experimental techniques to find out what babies actually know. It has been shown, for example, that, by the time they are born, babies are already primed to look for human facial features. If mothers stick out their tongues, babies will do likewise in a matching sequence. They will quickly go on to recognise different emotional expressions and other people's faces.[3]

Here is a comment by three specialists in infant development on this particular human given: "At first glance this ability to imitate might seem curious and cute but not deeply significant.

But if you think about it a minute, it is actually amazing. There are no mirrors in the womb: newborns have never seen their own face. So how do they know whether their tongue is inside or outside their mouth? There is another way of knowing what your face is like. As you read this, you probably have a good idea of your facial expression (we hope intense concentration leavened by the occasional smile). Try sticking out your tongue (in a suitably private setting). The way you know you've succeeded is through kinaesthesia, your internal feeling of your own body.

"In order to imitate, newborn babies must somehow understand the similarity between that internal feeling and the external face they see, a round shape with a long pink thing at the bottom moving back and forth. Newborn babies not only distinguish and prefer faces, they also seem to recognise that those faces are like their own face. They recognise that people are 'like me'. There is nothing more personal, more part of you, than this internal sense you have of your own body, your expressions and movements, your aches and tickles. And yet from the time we're born, we seem to link this deeply personal self to the bodily movements we can only see and not feel. Nature ingeniously gives us a jump start on the 'Other Minds' problem. We know, quite directly, that we are like other people and they are like us."[4]

Scientists have also shown that all normal babies are pre-primed to listen out for human language patterns and to pay attention to them. This quickly extends to more highly sophisticated levels of pattern matching. The genetic basis for the acquisition of language is a 'given' but, because the process is a metaphorical one, the baby has the flexibility to acquire the specific language of the country where it is raised. In other words, the instinctive template for language acquisition is matched up to whatever form the environment offers to ensure its completion. This innate ability to acquire language is therefore an analogical process. A young child born of English parents who move to Japan will have no trouble becoming fluent in Japanese as well as their mother tongue.

The importance of perception

Inborn patterns – templates – are so fundamental that no reality can exist without nature presetting them into organisms in the first place. We have been talking about pattern matching but in a way it is more accurate to talk about pattern *perception*. This is because it is not so much that we actually hold a template and seek the match of it, *we actually perceive reality through the template*. In other words, what we perceive are the *meanings* that we attribute to certain stimuli.

This has been demonstrated startlingly clearly in cases where cataracts have been removed from people blind from birth. Arthur Zajonc describes the outcome of one such operation: "In 1910, the surgeons Moreau and LePrince wrote about their successful operation on an eight-year-old boy who had been blind since birth because of cataracts. Following the operation, they were anxious to discover how well the child could see. When the boy's eyes were healed, they removed the bandages. Waving a hand in front of the child's physically perfect eyes, they asked him what he saw. He replied weakly, 'I don't know.' 'Don't you see it moving?' they asked. 'I don't know,' was his only reply. The boy's eyes were clearly not following the slowly moving hand. What he saw was only a varying brightness in front of him. He was then allowed to touch the hand as it began to move; he cried out in a voice of triumph: 'It's moving!' He could feel it move, and even, as he said, 'hear it move,' but he still needed laboriously to learn to see it move. Light and eyes were not enough to grant him sight. Passing through the now-clear black pupil of the child's eye, that first light called forth no echoing image from within. The child's sight began as a hollow, silent, dark and frightening kind of seeing. The light of day beckoned, but no light of mind replied within the boy's anxious, open eyes.

"The lights of nature and of mind entwine within the eye and call forth vision. Yet separately, each light is mysterious and dark. Even the brightest light can escape our sight."[5]

So, for everything we become aware of, there is a pre-existing, partially completed, inner template through which we literally organise the incoming stimuli and complete it in a way that gives it meaning. We propose that these metaphorical templates are the basis of all animal and human perception. Without them no world would exist. They organise consciousness and reality.

With this understanding we can see how crucial *meaning* is when helping people who are using inappropriate patterns through which to understand their reality. If a person has a mental template that the world owes them a living, for example, they need an input to correct that, otherwise they will always see their interactions with other people through this parasitic viewpoint and fall foul of the people around them. Likewise, someone who idealises the opposite sex is doomed to disappointment until a more realistic template is set in place.

The active ingredient in therapy and counselling is *always* around meaning – changing the meaning of something is what effective counsellors do.

Patterns seek completion

As children grow we can see patterns seeking completion in the environment all the time. It is clear to most parents, for example, that boys and girls have different instinctual orientations towards the world and these come out in the ways they play. An argument was put forward in the 1970s that boys' inclination to play with toy weapons and engage in rough and tumble games only occurred because they were conditioned or socialised into those behaviours. It then became politically incorrect to allow little boys to play with toy guns or bows and arrows. Preschool playgroups and infant schools banned such toys and games. But research carried out since has questioned this notion. One researcher found that, if boys are prevented from working through these templates, their self esteem suffers, whereas playing with toy guns can stimulate more creative and imaginative play and reduce aggression in the long run.[6] Some preschool nurseries now recognise this and no longer forbid play with toy weapons.

Another illustration of what happens when inner templates are not allowed to seek their fulfilment in the environment is the devastating story of a man reassigned from babyhood to live as a girl.

The procedure of reassigning sex in cases of ambiguity (a condition which can be caused by a number of genetic and hormonal irregularities) was largely established in the 1950s by psychologist Dr John Money of Johns Hopkins medical centre in Baltimore. He also invented the term 'gender identity'. Tragically, in the process of his work, he became convinced that all babies are psychosexually the same and that gender identity only emerges as a result of upbringing.

His chance to 'prove' this occurred when, in 1967, he was approached by a young couple whose baby boy twins had been obliged to undergo circumcision for medical reasons. The operation for one of them, John, had gone horribly wrong, and he had lost his penis.

The couple were persuaded to allow John to undergo surgical castration and the construction of feminine-style external genitalia at the age of 22 months – Dr Money believed that, after the age of two, gender reassignment was less likely to be a success. He told them that, once the operation had been carried out, and John had become Joan, they must never allow themselves to question their child's sex, in case doubts entered Joan's own mind as a result of their attitude.

Dr Money saw the twins once a year and asked the parents for reports of Joan's adjustment to her new sex. Mindful of the warning that they must not question their child's sex, it emerged later, the parents told him anything positive that they noticed and kept their considerable concerns to themselves.

In 1972, Money announced the procedure a resounding success at a meeting of the American Association for the Advancement of Science. This 'success' led to a worldwide acceptance in certain circumstances of such sex reassignment in babyhood.

The truth about Joan only became known when endocrinologist Dr Milton Diamond of the University of Hawaii, who had always taken issue with Money's position, managed in 1991 to track down and persuade 'Joan' to cooperate in his writing of a medical paper that set the record straight.

Joan by that time had been John again for many years. Writer John Colapinto spoke to John, his parents and his twin, and published the full story. It turned out that Joan had never adjusted to being a girl. From an early age she wanted to play with her twin brother's toys and ignored her own. She and her brother were both fascinated to see their father shave but were totally uninterested in their mother's make-up. It was noticeable that Joan walked like a boy and sat like a boy, legs apart, hand on knee. At the age of seven she had become convinced that she wasn't a girl and never had been, regardless of what anyone told her. When she thought of herself as grown up, she visualised a man with a moustache. At 11, her school noted her 'strongly masculine' interests. She was variously teased and rejected by other children.

As puberty approached, Joan was adamant, despite much pressure, that she would not have surgery to create a vaginal canal and only under extreme duress agreed to take female hormones. However, her male endocrine system was still intact and so she had small but definite breasts and padded hips as well as male gait and gestures and a deep voice. She was treated as a freak. At the age of 13 she stopped dressing as a girl and gave in to her instinctive desire to urinate in the standing position. Those attempting to treat her finally accepted the inevitable and her endocrinologist advised her father to tell Joan the truth. When he did, she experienced a gamut of predictably strong emotions but paramount was relief. She changed her name back to John, took male hormone treatment and had surgery to remove the breasts and reinstate a rudimentary penis.

Colapinto describes how, when asking 31-year-old John about his childhood, John's natural easy tones became angry and aggrieved and he proceeded to refer to himself as 'you'– "almost as if he is speaking about someone else altogether. Which, in a sense, he is". It was torture for John to recall what he terms the "psychological warfare" he had lived with in his mind.

Fortunately, his own story has a happy ending. He met and married a woman who already had three young children. The fathers had dumped her, and her first priority in a partner was a loving, caring nature. But the graphic lesson of his experience is a deeply salutary one.[7]

In couple counselling we are now beginning to realise the importance of understanding the differences between male and female templates and how this affects life on all levels. For example, men and women understand and address emotions differently, focus attention differently, may enjoy different types of conversation, express love for their children differently and are attracted to interests that often seem alien to the opposite sex. While there is much, of course, that is similar between the sexes, the divergences are there for good reason, and couples in trouble need to be helped to understand and respect them.

Emotions come first

Emotions are feelings which create distinctive psychobiological states, a propensity for action and simplified thinking styles.[8] They originate in a primitive part of the brain called the limbic system and it is here and in the thalamus that all basic patterns are stored.[9] This system is continually on the lookout for physical danger, monitoring information coming through our senses from the environment. It does all this prior to consciousness. There is an emergency short cut or fast track in the brain via which signals from our senses of potential threat reach a small structure in the limbic system, called the amygdala, before they reach the neocortex, the 'thinking' brain. This allows the 'emotional' brain to start to respond instantly to threat by triggering the 'fight or flight' reflex, and happens before the conscious brain knows anything about it.[10] In other words, we unconsciously interpret each stimulus in terms of "Does it represent a danger, or is it safe?" Perhaps even more fundamentally, "Is this something I can eat, or is it something that can eat me?" or, "Is it something I can approach or something I should get away from?" The conscious mind is presented with the end result of this analysis – what the emotional brain considers the significant highlights.

The information that comes into conscious awareness arrives up to half a second after the reality has been experienced unconsciously.[11] In other words, human beings experience conscious reality *after* it has actually occurred. It is what happens in that half second that is significant. Information, processed subconsciously at enormous speed, is compared to patterns already existing in the brain derived from previous experiences. On this basis the emotional brain decides whether what is happening now is threatening or non-threatening. Only after this filtering process has occurred is information sent 'up', if necessary, into consciousness.

Our conscious reality is always accompanied by emotions, ranging from very subtle to extremely strong. Emotions exist at a stage prior to language. They are the only language available to the subconscious mind for communicating the significance of patterns. It is the emotions that propel the higher cortex towards deciding an appropriate reaction to a particular situation. We become conscious of a feeling of anxiety, distrust, anger or attraction, and the higher neocortex then has the choice either of going along with it, or questioning it. That is when thoughts come into play.

In summary, if an emotion is strong, the signal will take the fast track route and trigger a response before the neocortex has had time to get involved. This is what happens when someone suddenly feels anxiety in a dark alley and runs away from a possible attacker in the shadows. It is also what happens in non-emergency situations, which certain individuals respond to *as if* they were emergencies because they haven't learned to adjust an inappropriate pattern from the past: for instance, when aggressive men automatically hit out at others before they have even had time to think what they are doing and why.

When the emotional arousal isn't quite so strong, the information can take the 'slow' track which involves the neocortex. In such circumstances, in the dark alley, it is the neocortex which may decide that the shadows are in fact empty and that the feelings and thoughts which they have prompted need modifying. At this point the conscious mind is acting as part of a feedback loop to the pattern-matching part of the mind, sending the message, "I think this pattern needs adjustment. I'm imagining things. Calm down."

It is the job of the conscious mind to discriminate, fill in the detail and offer a more intelligent analysis of the patterns offered up to it by the emotional brain. The 'either/or' logic of the emotional brain is its most basic pattern – one that goes right the way back to earliest life forms, unicellular creatures

– and this, crucially, is the foundation on which much of our behaviour and thinking rests.

The impact of our emotions

The fact that all emotions operate from a black and white, good or bad, perspective has had huge consequences for human evolution and history. The emotional brain is necessarily crude in its perceptions and the degree to which the fight or flight reflex is activated is the degree to which our thinking becomes polarised – more black or more white. When the emotional temperature rises, the emotional brain 'hijacks' (to use psychologist Daniel Goleman's memorable term) the higher, more recently evolved, cortex and very quickly begins to blank out the more subtle distinctions between individual stimuli. (When one is in danger of losing one's life, the ability to make fine discriminations must be shut off, so that we can act promptly and instinctively to take strong self preservative action.) So, with emotional arousal there is only a right or a wrong, all or nothing, black or white perception. Everything operates out of these two extremes.

If we look around the world today, wherever we see prejudice, discrimination, conflict, violence, torture and inhumane behaviour it is invariably accompanied by high levels of emotional arousal. The people doing these things are not different from the rest of us. Even the most intelligent person can behave like an ignoramus when emotionally aroused. And an atmosphere of continuous emotional arousal maintains ignorance because, when the higher neocortex is inhibited, no one can see the bigger picture. Black and white, emotional logic eliminates fine discrimination. As the old saying goes, "The coarse drives out the fine." Or, to put it more colloquially, high emotional arousal makes us stupid.

The higher neocortex evolved partly as a means to discriminate the thousands of shades of grey that exist between black and white. It has the capacity to modulate emotional responses – stand back and explore subtle implications and complexities, look at bigger contexts, analyse – but to do that it has to be able to interact with the emotional brain, *which is only possible if the emotional brain isn't too highly aroused.*

It is impossible to communicate normally with people who are too highly aroused. This is because, in their aroused state, they cannot process data contradictory to their black and white thinking. They cannot give attention to another viewpoint. High emotional arousal locks the attention mechanism, effectively putting the person into a trance state where they are confined to viewing the world through an inappropriate pattern or template, limiting their perception of reality. The best tactic when trying to communicate with a highly aroused person is to buy time and do whatever is necessary to bring their arousal level down first.

Counsellors and psychotherapists recognise that people suffering with anxiety, anger, addictive behaviour or depression are locked into a restricted view of reality. Their key role should be to open up their clients' view of reality. An effective counsellor should have the skills to disempower the templates that 'lock' their clients into disabling viewpoints and help them access more helpful ones so that they can operate out of a bigger pattern. This is known as reframing.

When we take account of brain physiology we can see that the fastest way to start helping a distressed person is to first calm them down, thus releasing their higher cortex from the mental paralysis caused by excessive emotional arousal. Clients are then more able to help themselves escape from their predicament.

Three vital principles

From what has been explained so far about brain function, we suggest that we can draw out three principles that are vital for therapists and counsellors to understand if they are to deal effectively with the most common emotional disorders, such as phobias, post-traumatic stress, anxiety, clinical depression and addictions:

- the brain works principally through an infinitely rich pattern-matching process. The clinical significance of this will be explained fully later.

- emotion comes before thought. All thought is 'fuelled' by emotion.

- the higher the emotional arousal, the more primitive the emotional/mental pattern that is engaged.

By studying therapy models with these fundamental principles in mind, we can more easily see their strengths and weaknesses. Any therapy that encourages emotional introspection, for example, is unlikely to be helpful for most common problems. This explains why efficacy studies repeatedly show that psychodynamic and Rogerian approaches to treating depression or anxiety may prolong or worsen the condition while any form of therapy which focuses on distraction will lift it.[12, 13, 14.]

Why cognitive therapy takes so long

A therapy method which research has shown to be one of the most successful for helping people suffering various forms of mental distress is cognitive therapy.[15] This therapy acknowledges the reciprocal interaction between cognition and emotion but operates out of a belief that changing thinking processes is the means by which to change inappropriate behaviour and emotions. The cognitive model was first formulated some decades ago. While it signified a brilliant step forward in therapeutic treatment methods, it is clearly not in alignment with what is now known about how the mind/body system works. This may explain why it can seem so slow and cumbersome. Clients are expected to need up to 20 sessions to make a dramatic improvement.

The thinking behind the method can, however, help us develop a model with more potential to achieve – and accelerate – therapeutic benefits for our clients.

Albert Ellis, the originator of rational emotive behaviour therapy, the first form of cognitive therapy, set out the structure of his 'thoughts cause emotional consequences' idea in his ABC model. (See diagram below.)

A ————————	B ————————	C
Activating agent, trigger event, or stimulus	Beliefs and thoughts. How the event is perceived and evaluated, which is a function of the client's core beliefs and thinking style	Consequences. Emotional response. How the client reacts to the stimulus

A stands for activating agent, the trigger event or stimulus in the environment that we are going to react to. **B** stands for the beliefs or thoughts we have about that event. **C** stands for the consequences of those beliefs, usually experienced as an emotion. So something happens, we interpret it through our thoughts and core beliefs, and we have an emotion. In other words our beliefs and thoughts give rise to our emotions. The cognitive model states simply that if we change our clients' thoughts and irrational beliefs, "shift their perceptions from those that are unrealistic and harmful to those that are more rational and useful",[16] then we will improve their emotional lives.

Aaron Beck, who founded cognitive restructuring therapy, concentrated primarily upon classifying and identifying what he regarded as the thought distortions which gave rise to all psychological disorders.[17] Over the decades cognitive therapists have continued to add to and further refine these thought styles and belief systems, which include, for instance, catastrophic thinking, overgeneralisation, personalising, sensationalising, fault-finding, 'musterbation', nominalising, self-righteousness and disqualifying positive life experiences.[18] We would suggest that *all* these thought distortions have one thing in common. They are all sub-categories of black and white polarised thinking. And black and white thinking *originates* in the emotional brain. This key insight is missing from cognitive therapy.

Ellis, Beck and other writers on cognitive approaches state or imply in their writings that, when problems occur, it is thinking that is defective. We would say that it is not. Thinking driven by the emotional brain is *always* all or nothing, black or white, fight or flight. The more emotionally aroused the brain becomes, the more it reverts to the primitive logic of either/or thinking.

The basic error in cognitive therapy is the idea that it is always thought that causes emotion. The method works because there is an important connection between thought and emotion (and because cognitive therapists concentrate on difficulties experienced in the here and now, not the past, which is the key to solving problems). But, by focusing on the idea that irrational thinking causes emotional disturbance, cognitive therapists are less likely to be as effective as those who look at their clients from the perspective of the human givens, which fully takes into account current knowledge about the way the brain works. It is a given that any form of emotional arousal makes us more single minded – and hence more simple-minded.

APET model: cognitive therapy with a twist

By contrast with the conventional ABC cognitive therapy model, introduced in the 1970s, the APET model (see below) used by human givens psychotherapists in the UK presents a more psychologically sophisticated and physiologically accurate view of mind/body functioning.

The **A** in APET again stands for activating agent, a stimulus from the environment, just as in the cognitive model. Information about that stimulus, taken in through our senses, is processed through the pattern-matching part of the mind, hence the **P**, which in turn gives rise to an emotion, **E**, which in turn may inspire certain thoughts, **T**. (Alternatively it may not, because a lot of our pattern matching is unconscious and does not result in thought.)

A ————	**P** —————	**E** ————	**T**
Activating agent, trigger event, or stimulus.	Pattern matching	Emotional arousal	Thought and conditioned beliefs

That there is emotional accompaniment to *all* perceptions may not seem obvious. However, when the emotional accompaniment is *not* there it stands out in bizarre ways. For example, Capgras' syndrome, which results from brain damage to connections between the temporal lobes and the amygdala, has the effect of making sufferers think that people they love and care about are impostors.[19] Although the parts of the brain that pattern match and can recognise individuals are still working, the damage prevents the integration of all of the emotional associations, feelings and meanings associated with, for instance, one's parents or spouse. These don't get activated and, in the absence of such feelings, the person's brain jumps to the conclusion: "This person *can't* be my father/mother/husband/wife!"

Normally people don't give a second thought to the feelings that accompany seeing their parents or partners because the brain accepts those feelings as normal, and doesn't bring them into consciousness. All unremarkable emotions are neutralised in this way – a fact that makes the phenomenon difficult to observe until an exception demonstrates it, as with this particular type of brain damage. People with Capgras' syndrome are severely disabled by the ensuing lack of emotional connection to their perceptions.

So, even though the most common of perceptions have feelings associated with them, we only become aware of feelings and our thoughts about feelings when they are somehow unexpected – surprising. Surprise is the common element.

When the neocortex is not too emotionally aroused it can employ ever more subtle evaluation procedures. The neocortex is in a state of continual flux from second to second, minute to minute and hour to hour.[20] This has to be so, to enable us to be adaptable creatures, capable of going with the flow of ever changing realities in the environment. The neocortex is nature's solution to the need for adaptable responses. It makes us a gift of instinctive patterns that are not totally programmed and, furthermore, gives us the ability to add to these patterns almost infinitely.

Every researcher and writer on the subject describes this incredibly complex organ, the neocortex, in awed tones. It has literally billions of potential neuronal connections and the almost inconceivable ability to continually remodel itself according to the richness of input coming in through the senses from the environment. It continually makes new connections, strengthening valuable ones and dissolving old ones that it no longer finds useful. It can hold on to and store whatever information is pertinent to its current reality and use that store of connections to modify the emotional responses received from the emotional brain – a complex fine-tuning operation. It is this continual refining of the metaphorical pattern-matching process that allows us to discriminate ever more accurately between the polarised extremes of the emotional brain's black and white responses.

Using the APET model

Using the APET approach (activating stimulus processed through the pattern-matching part of the mind, giving rise to emotion, giving rise to thought) provides many more points of intervention than simply helping clients to challenge their belief systems directly, as in cognitive therapy.

Human givens therapists are acutely aware, for example, of how influencing the activating agent, the **A** in APET, can dramatically improve people's lives. If someone is depressed because they are being bullied at work, they can be encouraged to think about options such as changing jobs.

One young married woman suffered vomiting fits every time her critical and somewhat interferring mother-in-law visited, which was very frequently. She was encouraged (by JG) to be sick in front of her on the kitchen floor, and then rush to her room, leaving her mother-in-law to clear up. This had the effect of changing the frequency of the mother-in-law's visits (the activating agent) and gave the younger woman back control in her own home. The vomiting stopped.

The principle of changing the activating agent can also be seen at work in a social context. For example, in New York in 1980 a remarkable project to clean up the city's subway system got underway in the belief that the impetus to engage in certain kinds of antisocial behaviour comes not from particular types of people but from the nature of the environment. Billions of dollars were invested in cleaning and rebuilding the subway stations, and removing all graffiti from trains or replacing trains that were beyond recovery with shiny new, *clean* ones. The instant any graffiti appeared on a surface it was removed. If a train was defaced it was taken out of service and returned to its pristine state. Within six years the clean-up was complete. The same zero tolerance policy was then enacted on crime. Even minor misdemeanours were prosecuted. The crime rate in New York, even for serious offences, fell dramatically, all because, when a signal goes out from the environment that 'this is not a place to behave in a criminal way', the brain pattern to behave antisocially is not elicited.[21] In other words, the activating agent had been changed.

Human givens therapists are also aware of the pattern-matching process in the linguistic phenomenon known as nominalisation, when an abstract noun is produced by taking a verb or adjective and turning it into a noun. A politician might change the verb *to modernise* into the noun *modernisation*. He will then say things like "what we need is *modernisation*", as though it were something concrete that you could buy, see or touch. These are words that hypnotise both the listener *and* the speaker because, to make sense of them, you have to go on an inner search to find a pattern of what they mean to you ... because they always mean something different to whoever hears them. (This is the **P** in APET) That is why they are stock-in-trade words of politicians, preachers and gurus.

Examples of negative nominalisations – words and phrases – include: *black cloud, evil, misery, depressed, worthless, useless, hopeless, fear, gloom, low self-esteem*. If therapists are not aware of the pattern-matching process in themselves, such words can lead them to identify closely with the misery of their clients.

Examples of positive nominalisations include: *happiness, love, creativity, integrate, resources, joy, insight, learnings, power, awareness, spirit, truth, beauty, consciousness, enlightenment, possibilities*. Although these words are typically used by gurus and politicians to manipulate people, many of them can be used by therapists and counsellors to send clients on a constructive, useful, inner search to help them access more useful patterns of behaviour.

Thought patterns *can* be changed directly and consciously of course, provided the person isn't too emotionally aroused. The new thought is fed back into the emotional brain and helps the moderation or change of inappropriate pattern matching and its emotional consequences. But, when a person is highly emotionally aroused, it is far more effective to calm down their emotions first so that the neocortex can function more intelligently. They can then more easily see all the shades of grey between the emotionally driven black and white frames of reference they are stuck in.

Cognitive therapy delivered from the APET model produces faster results and also dispenses with the need for the complex language which cognitive therapists have evolved to teach patients how to classify and challenge their thinking. Once a person is emotionally calmed down they can be given the information they need, either directly or through metaphor, to help them see their situation from multiple viewpoints. What is happening in effect is that they are learning to employ a finer, more discriminating pattern – a more accurate representation of reality.

Very many complementary and behavioural therapists already recognise the importance of relaxation in calming people down so that they can engage more effectively with their higher neocortex.[22] The APET model offers a unifying theoretical basis for this and other successful therapy approaches. For example, with an understanding of the metaphorical pattern-matching function of the brain, and of how our instinctive templates are first programmed in the REM state, in the womb and after birth, we can see how cognitive therapy connects to hypnotherapy and guided imagery. All forms of hypnosis and guided imagery directly access the REM state, helping clients reprogramme patterns of response that are unhelpful to them.[23]

Until recently hypnosis was treated with awe, incredulity or hostility within the psychotherapeutic community. Practitioners either seize on it enthusiastically or deny and reject it. But research by a leading exponent, psychiatrist Milton H Erickson, and others strongly indicates that hypnosis is the single most powerful psychotherapeutic tool available to us. It is so powerful precisely because it accesses the state of consciousness in which nature programmes the brain *and can reprogramme it*.[24] Unfortunately, however, like any powerful tool, it can be misused – and frequently is.

The APET model also integrates metaphor therapy and storytelling with other effective approaches. When a more useful metaphorical pattern is offered to clients, they have the capacity, through the brain's own pattern matching process, to decipher the metaphor for themselves, with the result that their solution is 'owned' by them rather than imposed on them by the therapist. Because it is the clients themselves who have made the connection, the connections are all the more 'hard-wired' and more firmly established. The method also enables rapport to be maintained because, if a client doesn't feel that a particular story or metaphor is relevant to them, they can just let it go past them, without feeling they have rejected 'advice' from the therapist. (Often, however, the meaning of a pertinent story will penetrate at a later date.)

Reframing, widely recognised as a core skill in effective counselling, works in the same way. All human development involves reframing whereby we learn to see another aspect or dimension to a situation. A reframe replaces a pattern that has become deficient in useful relevance and offers up a richer, more appropriate one that opens up the models of reality in our brains so that we can see further possibilities that we hadn't previously realised were there.

All effective therapy involves reframing. The determining factor in a person's happiness is not just what happens to them in life but how they interpret experience, or how they 'frame', or put meaning to, life events. Some 'frames' empower us and some disempower us. When someone unconsciously assumes that their way of perceiving reality is the only way, then a major shift can occur when another view is unexpectedly demon-strated to them. After such a reframe it is virtually impossible to maintain the problem behaviour in the same way.

As well as providing an organic basis for understanding and integrating the active ingredients within potent therapeutic methodologies used today, the APET model also provides a clear theoretical understanding of why certain psychological condi-tions, such as depression, addictions, anxiety disorders, post traumatic stress (PTSD), obsessional behaviour and phobias arise. With this understanding we can look afresh at such debilitating conditions and see how they could be better treated.

Trauma symptoms

It is easy to see the pattern matching connection in conditions such as traumatic stress, where situations that are not traum-atic but have some basic similarity to a past traumatic event, trigger off in the individuals concerned intense inappropriate fear reactions.

What is happening in the brain is this. As explained earlier, incoming sensory information passes to the structure in the brain called the thalamus, which then directs it to the amyg-dala. This has the role of deciding the emotional significance of the signals received and how to react. Normally, at this stage the signals are formed into a sensory memory and then passed on to the hippocampus and cortex, where they are formed into a verbal memory.

When, however, a traumatic event occurs, such as a serious fire, car crash or rape, the emotional strength of the signal may be so strong that an overload occurs and the sensory memories become a separate template encoded and accessed via the amygdala.[25] However, the amygdala continues to pattern match it against current events. Because pattern matching at this level is crude, just one or two pieces of emotionally arousing sensory information similar to that experienced during the trauma are sufficient to trigger the amygdala to fire off the alarm reaction. The fight or flight reflex is activated and the person re-enters the state of alarm they experienced when they were first traumatised. If they were hit by a car, for example, even seeing a car on TV or in a photograph can bring on flash-backs and fear. If they were involved in a shooting incident, any loud bang, even a door slamming, can reduce them to a terrified heap on the floor.

Because the trauma memory is stored in a pre-verbal state, it is re-experienced in sensory form. Thus the common symp-toms of post traumatic stress disorder: intrusive memories, flashbacks, repetitive nightmares, anger, anxiety states, hyper-vigilance, exaggerated startle response, avoidance behaviour etc. Because the memory is pre-verbal, often affected individuals will have no idea why certain seemingly innocuous situations cause them to have panic attacks. One man, for instance, exper-ienced intense panic and fear whenever he went into petrol stations to fill up his car. When he was helped to link the smell of petrol with the strong fumes of diesel fuel that had assaulted his senses when his motorboat capsized and he was plunged into freezing water, he was able to change the pattern of his response.[26] A woman, who had experienced an armed raid at work could not go into her kitchen at home without panic. She too was able to change her response when she was helped to recall that, while she had lain terrified on the floor during the raid, a kettle was coming to the boil in the office kitchen next door.[27]

It is clear that, because the brain is a pattern-matching organ, there is a double-bind situation here, both for the traumatised victim and for the counsellor. If the victim seeks to recall, or is encouraged to talk about, the traumatic event, off goes the alarm. An emotional charge inhibits the higher neocortex from functioning and the person is reduced to jelly. This means that, without the brain's normal feedback mechanism operating through the higher cortex, the traumatic memory is further reinforced, thereby deepening the trauma.

This is why counselling or therapy methods which require an individual to talk through or relive the event in any way that engages the emotions do not work – as research has now shown.[28,29]

Most forms of critical incident debriefing (now widely offered after major life-threatening events, or where horrific deaths have been witnessed in accidents, murders or natural disasters) encourage people to express their emotions about the traumatic event and recreate in detail their experiences – resulting commonly in the aggravation of symptoms. Only a minority of people suffer post traumatic stress disorder after traumatic experiences. Yet those who are at greatest risk of developing post traumatic stress disorder are those who are most likely to be harmed by that counselling approach. (The only debriefing methods found beneficial are those which involve no intense reliving of what happened.[30])

Working from the APET model we can clearly see why this is so. Traumatised people need help to transform the trauma imprint into an ordinary memory in the higher cortex so that the inappropriate pattern matching stops. It is necessary to access the more objective intelligence in the neocortex so that it can evaluate the imprint, see that it no longer represents a threat to life, and modify it. This has to be done without firing off the fight or flight response.

Once the information is processed beyond the amygdala into narrative memory, it becomes a *normal* memory, albeit an unpleasant one, and no longer signifies a threat that the brain must remain vigilant against, keeping an individual in an unnatural state of high arousal.

Furthermore, when the trauma template is released, attention capacity is freed up. A person literally becomes more intelligent again because the data-processing capability of the brain is no longer working to hold that pattern of trauma locked in place.

There is a very simple and swift therapeutic procedure for neutralising trauma which enables arousal level to be kept down while the memory is recalled, so that the information can be transferred into, and evaluated by, the neocortex. It is variously known as VK (visual kinaesthetic) dissociation or the fast phobia cure, and involves taking an individual while in a deeply relaxed state very swiftly backwards and forwards several times through the trauma, but at one remove – as if they were watching themselves on a screen. Clinical experience shows that it works reliably for both phobias and post traumatic stress disorder.

The technique can also usefully be applied to accelerate recovery from other disorders such as panic attacks, agoraphobia and obsessive compulsive disorders. It is widely taught around the country to health professionals[31] and described in detail in *Organising Ideas Monograph No. 5*.[32]

Phobias

The most successful methods of dealing with phobias are those which do not concern themselves with the cause but which work, in effect, to change the pattern in the brain which links fear with the object of the phobia. Absolutely anything can become the cause of a phobia. Impressive Greek inspired names have been coined to describe a great number of them, for instance nephophobia (fear of clouds), aulophobia (fear of flutes), nomatophobia (fear of names) and neophobia (fear of novelty).[33]

Some phobias do have an original cause, such as a fear of enclosed spaces after being trapped in a lift or locked in a broom cupboard during a game as a child, although the cause is not always consciously recalled by the sufferer. Others have no such direct explanation. In either case it is necessary to reduce the emotional arousal experienced in the presence of the feared object. This has successfully been achieved by behavioural methods such as desensitisation (where the phobic individual is asked to construct a hierarchy of fears and imagine experiencing each in turn over a period of time, starting with the least frightening, while in a deeply relaxed state). Sometimes the individual is asked to experience the situations for real, having been taught quick relaxation methods to apply should panic arise. More speedy is the method known as flooding, in which the individual is exposed in a controlled manner to the object of their fears from the outset. Although high anxiety is experienced in this method, so is the fact that the anxiety quite quickly falls and that the fear – usually of dying from the panic – is unfounded.

Also highly effective is the fast phobia cure, mentioned in the previous section. Here, while in a deeply relaxed state, the sufferer is taken quickly backwards and forwards through occasions that have caused them terror, as if watching them on a screen (whether these are real life instances or seeing the feared object on screen or in books) and is then encouraged to visualise instances of successfully facing those fears in the future.

All such methods give the neocortex a chance to re-evaluate and change the pattern of response.

Panic attacks

A panic attack is the setting off of the fight or flight reflex, the emergency reaction which prepares the body to deal with physical danger. Nowadays most of us are rarely in the presence of life-threatening events and yet many people experience panic attacks, usually resulting from a progressive rising in background stress levels until the point where one more stress – the straw that breaks the camel's back – sets off the alarm reaction triggering the fight or flight reflex.

When this first occurs, not surprisingly people don't understand what's happening to them, why their heart is pounding, why they are sweating, why their breathing is accelerated, and so they jump to the alarming conclusion that something must be seriously amiss with their body. This causes a further rise in the alarm reaction, a further release of adrenaline, and even more intensified panic symptoms.

When we experience extreme alarm during a panic attack the brain, naturally enough, is desperately scanning the environment to find out where the threat to its survival – as the amygdala sees it – might be. Not surprisingly, in many people, an association is made with an element in the environment where the panic attack occurs.

If it first occurs in a supermarket, for example, the emotional imprint may lead an individual to avoid supermarkets in future, even though the panic attack was caused not by the supermarket but by raised stress levels. Once the faulty association has been made, the fight or flight response will continue to fire off every so often, pattern matching to any environment that has similar elements in it to that of the supermarket: a post office, a bank, anywhere with bright lights or crowds or queues. People thus affected may then progressively avoid all these places and gradually the noose of agoraphobia grips them, hindering their interaction with life itself. In the worst cases, they become confined to home, terrified of the outside world.

A combination of relaxation, behavioural therapy and cognitive therapy is useful in treating this condition. Sufferers are taught to calm themselves down and progressively re-engage with life. It can take many sessions of therapy and practice. This whole process, however, is accelerated if we first detraumatise (using the fast phobia cure) the memories of their most frightening panic attacks. As a result the brain will cease to pattern match in a destructive way when they enter each new, previously frightening, situation. Once the disabling emotional memories are processed, people can progress more rapidly through the situations that they had previously been avoiding.

Obsessive compulsive disorder

Obsessive compulsive disorder (OCD), can take many forms but is most often seen in repeated washing and checking behaviours. Again, often the background trigger is raised stress levels, which may be due to anything from physical illness, a fright, not getting enough sleep to business worries, a relationship breakdown or stress around examinations.[34] Some people have a propensity to develop this disorder in response to raised stress levels.

OCD is a complex neuropsychiatric process characterised by a homogenous core of three main symptoms:

1. intrusive, forceful and repetitive thoughts, images, or sounds that dwell in the mind without the possibility of rejecting them
2. imperative needs to perform motor or mental acts
3. doubt or chronic questioning about major or minor matters.[35]

Sufferers of OCD may be, in effect, responding to post hypnotic suggestions implanted accidentally by environmental factors – they lose track of time and forget how long they have been performing the obsessive behaviour, or whether they even have, and so start all over again. Losing track of time and amnesia are common hypnotic phenomena.

Clearly a pattern match is fired up in the brain and then embedded deeper and deeper by repetition – much as in addiction behaviour. Changing such deeply entrenched patterns is not easy but is possible in many cases and working from the APET model offers multiple ways in which to go about it.

One key step, for example, is to help the person take a step back so that they can observe themselves and their behaviour. They can thus separate their core identity from the problem and recognise that *the OCD behaviour is not who they are.* (Indeed one can sometimes effect a fairly dramatic recovery in many conditions by simply making that distinction very clear to the person.)

Depression

It has been shown that depression is associated with memory bias – either a better memory for negative events or a poorer memory for positive events and experiences. This has led to the widely accepted theory that the onset of depression somehow facilitates access to negative memories which, once recalled, serve to exacerbate and lengthen the depression.[36] The more that we go back over the stories in our lives the more we are increasing and programming in the saliency of those patterns. Somebody in depression who is continually resurrecting negative life experiences is programming those negative templates into their unconscious mind. Therefore new stimuli coming in to their conscious minds, before ever reaching consciousness, are being matched up and scanned by negative templates to draw out what is negative in those experiences. Perceptions are continuously, subconsciously biased by the negative templates that are programmed in as a result of negative rumination.

In cognitive therapy, people may be asked to challenge their conviction that everything they do is always wrong or hopeless by recalling successes and achievements. But the memory bias and reinforcing of negative patterns makes it hard for a depressed person to recall good memories, so it isn't easy for them to generate a more positive attitude to life, however much they are willed to. Therapy based on the APET model, working from the human givens, can take a more diverse and creative approach to shifting unhelpful patterns, particularly through the use of metaphor and story, which impact on the unconscious mind more directly and powerfully than reason.[37] (An explanation of the cycle of depression and how to break it is contained in *Organising Idea Monograph No. 3* – see page 59).

In the same way human givens counselling has a much increased chance of helping people with addictions and anger disorders.

Placebo – nocebo

The placebo response has baffled scientists and puzzled human beings since perhaps the dawn of civilisation. It was certainly referred to by Chaucer in his writings. The word comes from *placebo domino*, "I will please the Lord", a term that was associated with travelling friars who demanded money from poor people to say prayers for their dead – in effect, a form of emotional blackmail. For centuries the word placebo was a term of abuse. But gradually doctors started using it to describe the response whereby some patients recovered from illnesses even when medicine was ineffectual, as if some kind of faith healing had taken place.

One of the functions of modern double-blind trials is to find out whether a medicine is the cause of a person's cure or whether they may get better because of a doctor's implicit 'suggestion' that a medicine will work. Double-blind means that neither the doctors nor the patients in a trial know who is receiving the active treatment and who the placebo, and somebody neutral hands out the pills. For when doctors know which pill contains the genuine drug, their own belief system somehow transmits to the patients and the patients often improve because of that.

The remarkable thing, however, is that even with the most stringent double-blind trials there is still an effect on the control group. A significant number of the control group invariably get better, even when taking an inert substance, compared with those given an active medicinal ingredient. To be considered effective a new drug must be significantly superior in effect to the placebo response experienced by the control group. (What hasn't been realised till relatively recently, however, is that there is a placebo effect to active medicines too.[38])

Increasingly in recent years, some scientists and clinicians have been asking whether there is any way to harness the placebo response. Instead of just dismissing it as an embarrassing finding, the thinking is that the placebo effect must surely reflect an innate capacity within human beings for self healing: if we could find a way of tapping into this, we might be able to tap into nature's own way of healing itself. This might open the door to powerful new treatments with no side effects.

Indeed it *is* possible to tap into the placebo effect. We would suggest that pattern matching – the P in APET – is at its basis and can help us understand the mind/body connections involved. Three conditions must be fulfilled before a placebo can work. There must be a pattern that can be matched to, however crudely (we have seen how even just one or two elements of similarity is enough); the treatment must seem plausible enough for the brain to interpret it as capable of bringing about a healing reaction; and the emotions must be engaged – the individual must completely accept that the treatment could work.

So, the placebo, first and foremost, generates a pattern that corresponds to a pattern the brain already knows. Matching to this pattern gives the brain the ability to alter the body's reactions. When a person is offered a pill (dummy or otherwise) to cure a headache, the pattern being matched to is "I've had headaches before and I feel better when I take a pill/ this colour pill/this shape of pill" or whatever.

When the treatment is a novel one, for instance a treatment for cancer, the patient's belief in the plausibility of its working must be stronger, as there is no past success to match to. (The pattern to which the brain must match is one of wellbeing.) It may be sufficient that the patient trusts the doctors and places great store by the fact that they have international reputations or that they successfully treated a family member or friend.

For the placebo effect to work there must be only one pattern for the brain to try to match to. The pattern must be "This can make me feel better", and there can be no competing patterns, such as "This may work or it may not". For the brain to focus on the one pattern, the emotions must be aroused, creating in effect a trance state of belief and conviction. Expectation, desire for the treatment to work, faith in the doctor and a sense of urgency, for instance, all help arouse the emotions and create the desired focusing of attention. When a credible pattern is focused on with a level of emotional arousal that locks the attention on to the required result, the brain then does all it can to pattern match to that result.

One of us (JG) often tells the tale of his own experience of a placebo response which bears out the above. He had heard from a fairly reliable source that aspirin could stop a hangover. "As I was very curious to know whether this could be true, I promised myself that I would try it out when appropriate. But I don't drink very much, and very rarely too much. This meant my frustration levels were building up, the more I was denied an opportunity to put the method to the test. Eventually, however, after a family celebration, I managed to drink enough to cause a hangover. So I eagerly took an aspirin and went to bed.

"I woke up the next morning on cloud nine – not a trace of a hangover. I felt as though I were walking on air. I felt similar to the way that some of my heroin addict patients describe feeling after taking heroin. In fact I suspect that is exactly what I *was* experiencing; the release of my body's own endogenous heroin, namely endorphins."

If we look at the mechanics of what occurred here for JG we can see a clear illustration of how the placebo response works. First there was a credible theory – that taking an aspirin could prevent a hangover – but there was also a frustration build up: a build up of emotional arousal. So the placebo effect was triggered and he woke the next morning after a release of endorphins which made him feel very positive indeed.

However, the story doesn't end there, as JG explains: "Subsequent to that first experiment I again took an aspirin on another occasion when I thought I might have a hangover. But this time it didn't work! The difference was that the second time I took the aspirin there was no emotional arousal and my attention was not focused on the outcome."

The emotional arousal and focusing of attention is enormously important. It explains why, for instance, some people who attend accident and emergency departments for crippling headaches respond to placebo tablets.[39] Being in an accident and emergency department is an unusual experience. Just being there sends a powerful message to the emotional brain that there is something seriously wrong, which raises emotional levels and locks attention on to whatever tablet is given. The tablet is a physical metaphor that seeks a pattern match. The pattern match provokes an endorphin release that relieves pain.

Other research has shown that, if a placebo is given by injection, it is more effective than if it is given by tablet.[40] This is because an injection is seen as stronger medicine. Also, smaller tablets have been found more powerful than standard tablets, probably because patients are subliminally influenced to believe that they must be receiving a very concentrated essence of the 'medicine'. This unconsciously focuses their attention even more. Such methods give the rituals more credibility.

The placebo effect is an enormously powerful effect, as we have seen, but it is definitely not magic. Even when all the conditions are right, as described above, healing cannot occur if, for instance, a cancer is too advanced or the immune system is not strong enough. This along with any lack of conviction explains why placebos often do *not* work.

A reverse to the placebo effect also exists. In this, known as the 'nocebo' effect or medical hexing, patients' conditions worsen as a result of doctors unintentionally conveying negative suggestions to which the patients respond. Simple instances might be "I haven't had a patient respond to this treatment yet, but ...", "I don't know much about this treatment personally ...", "Well, it might be worth a try", "This doesn't work for 40 per cent of people." Whenever a doctor focuses a patient's attention on a possibly negative outcome, even with a throwaway remark, the emotion the remark arouses in the patient's brain will lock attention on to it and tend to bring about the negative outcome. That is why it is important that doctors are careful with the language they use when giving prognoses or life expectancy projections. In very many cases their patients may fulfil the predictions that have been suggested to them.

So, to recap, the placebo response is most likely to work when a credible ritual is offered with positive endorsement from the relevant therapist which raises the patient's expectations of improvement or cure. A placebo is an undifferentiated metaphor. Once the instinctive, unconscious, emotional brain has its attention mechanism locked on to a pattern, it does everything it can to try to complete that pattern – to find a match to it.

It has been shown, unsurprisingly, that those who are most susceptible to hypnosis are also most likely to respond to well delivered placebos. The credible ritual is a metaphor. It can be a physical metaphor like a tablet, injection or procedure, or it can be mental metaphor, like a phrase, theory or story. Tablets etc. are fairly crude metaphors. The giving of one doesn't convey much guidance about how the patient should use it to mobilise their own immune system. A story, however, especially when delivered while a patient is in trance (a focused state of attention) can provide a disguised means of giving highly detailed instructions for kick-starting the immune system.

The following case is an example of how one of us (IT) used this means to help a depressed woman whose feet were deformed by dozens of painful verrucas. One of the verrucas was as big as a 50p piece and some days she could barely stand with the pain.

Over the previous years she had attended chiropodists at different hospitals and received a variety of treatments, even surgery, all to no avail. But, within a few weeks of putting her into a trance and telling her this story, her verrucas had gone and her depression had lifted. Three months later, her feet were completely smooth.

ONCE UPON a time there was a wonderful land ruled over by a wise and popular king. He kept his people safe from enemies and helped them prosper and thus he earned their respect. But, as happens, the king died and his only daughter inherited the kingdom and became queen. At first all went well for she possessed her father's wisdom and worked hard for the good of the people who consequently loved her.

Then calamity struck. Alien barbarians invaded the southern regions of the kingdom and built ugly castles from where they sallied forth, pillaging the surrounding country-side making life unbearable for the people. The young queen didn't know what to do as the invaders drained the lifeblood of her country causing more and more pain and the people lost their spirit.

As the months and years passed the invaders entrenched

themselves deeper and deeper and the queen grew more desperate.

One day an old warrior rode up to her palace and begged an audience. The queen bade him welcome and asked him what he wanted.

"You are a good queen beset by troubles," he said. "And I am here to help you. The troubles come about because, unlike your father, who I knew as a young man, you are not skilled in the arts of war."

"Then what must I do to rid my country of these evil parasites?" the queen asked.

"It is not difficult," said the old warrior. "With your permission, I can do it on your behalf using the tried and tested techniques of siege warfare. But you must give me command of your people to do it."

The queen felt she had nothing to lose and the old warrior set about mobilising her people and turning them into armies, one for each castle. He showed each army how to surround the barbarian castles – lay siege to them – and stressed how important it was that the occupants were prevented from getting any sustenance or nutriment from the surrounding countryside.

"You will soon see," said the old warrior, "that the enemy will either die off in the castles or retreat from whence they came."

And so it was. Soon the land was cleared of the invaders and their ugly castles quickly decayed or were destroyed. Peace and prosperity returned to the kingdom.

The queen thanked the old warrior and rewarded him well and he settled nearby in case she ever needed him again.

The story is clearly a metaphor for the client's problem and for the solution (her immune system needed to "mobilise" itself for a big effort and "lay siege" to the verrucas). She had no conscious recollection of the story after coming out of trance.[41]

Not only does the pattern-matching concept open up an

understanding of how the placebo effect works but, as in the above example, it explains why its conscious use as a psycho-therapeutic procedure is often so effective.

Nocebo counselling

Once one understands the APET model it is easy to see why some counselling is ineffective or harmful. Counsellors are often trained to encourage emotionally arousing introspection in their clients about what might be 'causing' their problems. The emotional arousal this produces locks the client's attention on negative patterns of thought and behaviour. This will lead, almost inevitably, to the development of negative rumination and the cycle of depression can set in. The process, however unintentional, can, therefore, accurately be characterised as nocebo therapy.

When counsellors encourage people to remember, and get emotional about, negative life experiences – bringing to the fore destructive patterns – they are actually going against nature's inclination to promote survival, health and wellbeing. And that's why some people say they go to see their counsellor feeling miserable and come out feeling suicidal. The essence of good therapy, on the other hand, is placebo therapy – focusing clients' attention on problem solving and solutions.

Metaphor, storytelling and learning

If the ideas set out in this monograph are right and the brain is fundamentally concerned with matching metaphorical patterns, it follows that this is the most wonderful natural tool for learning. Learning is a process of refining patterns of perception built upon a foundation of instinctive patterns. All learning is an extension of existing patterns in the student. We are referring here not to learning facts by rote, in effect just storing up a series of bits of information, but to real learn-ing – interacting more effectively with the environment, and developing the ability to discriminate and discern a greater subtlety of the patterns therein and how they connect up with our own inner perceptions. If real learning is about the ability to discriminate patterns, as counsellors or teachers our aim must be to introduce a new more constructive pattern to clients'/students' brains, or refine an existing one, so that they can see reality more accurately.

The way creative breakthroughs are made in science illustrates the power of this approach. The breakthrough 'ah hah' experience comes when scientists recognise that a pattern which works in one area of reality can also be applied in another. They take a pattern that explains one phenomenon and use it as a metaphor to explain what is going on in a different phenomenon.

For example, if we take current theories of light, and the metaphors that are used to explain them, on the one hand we have the theory that light is a stream of particles travelling like *bullets* in sequence in a beam. And, on the other, we have a metaphor which explains other aspects of light as a *wave*. Both these metaphors have the capacity to explain a peculiarity of light – that sometimes it can appear to behave as a wave and sometimes like a sequence of bullets.

One of the most famous metaphorical insights concerns Kekule's discovery of the structure of the benzene ring: one of the most important discoveries in the history of chemistry. He had been trying for years to solve the problem of the molecular structure of benzene. Then one afternoon, as he was puzzling over the problem, he began to doze. He saw atoms gambolling before his eyes. Then he saw larger structures in long rows, twisting and entwining in a snakelike motion, until they looked just like snakes. One of the 'snakes' proceeded to seize its own tail. He awoke with a jolt to realise that the structure of benzene must be a closed ring – a solution suggested to him by the image of the snake swallowing its own tail.

Conveying new, desired patterns in a metaphor or story is perhaps the most effective way of all to refine patterns (although there are other effective methods, such as modelling desired behaviours). Psychiatrist Milton H Erickson, whom we regard as the most significant clinician and psychotherapist of the 20th century, was a master storyteller who put this skill to good effect in his work. Often the teachers who most influence pupils' education are those who use anecdotes and stories to make their lessons come alive. In a counselling training context, we ourselves use stories and case histories to illustrate our theoretical principles in order to bring those principles alive. All good communicators use stories for that reason.

If clients are missing some piece of the jigsaw puzzle of life we could offer them a story about another client with a similar problem and how *their* behaviour changed, conveying the desired new pattern in an indirect way, or we could tell an appropriate traditional story. The world's stories, oral and written, contain a fantastic cornucopia of wonderful patterns which chart the possibilities of understanding ourselves more profoundly and help us engage with the world more fruitfully.

Somebody who is struggling with an addiction might benefit from hearing the ancient Greek myth about Odysseus who, on his way home to Greece after the battle of Troy, had to pass the island of the sirens. He had been told by the enchantress Circe that all sailors who passed that island were lured to their death on the rocks if they heard the sirens' song. But she had also told him a way to hear the sirens' magical music and survive. She told him to order his sailors to put softened beeswax in their ears, to stop them hearing the singing, and then have them tie him fast to the mast, giving them instructions that, no matter how much he urged or pleaded with them to turn the boat towards the island, they should merely bind him faster and continue on their course, past the island. This was done. When Odysseus heard the sirens' song, he wanted with every cell of his body to go to the island but, because he had fore-warned his crew, they ignored his signals to change direction, bound him even more tightly to the mast, and eventually they passed the island. Odysseus was released by the crew, enormously grateful that he had been enabled to survive – and that he had escaped being dragged to his doom.

This powerful metaphorical template with all its allusions and implications can be used to show how a drug or addictive experience may be extremely seductive and yet destructive. It also metaphorically sets in place a template for how people can reorganise their internal resources to fight it.

This form of learning can be used if appropriate in conjunction with cognitive behavioural approaches to increase the chances of a successful outcome.

To recap, to help educate clients who are stuck we have to help them understand what is blocking them from getting their needs met. This is done through refining their patterns of perception, helping incorporate these patterns into their own perceptual apparatus and creating a more healthy, outward focus on life. If those patterns are not already active, the job of the counsellor is to help draw them forth, thus providing a stronger and more accurate lens through which the client can perceive reality. Using metaphor is one of the most powerful ways this can be done.

This whole process can be greatly speeded up by using nature's own tool for accelerated learning. This is the state of consciousness known as REM sleep, where, as mentioned, in the foetus and early months of life, nature lays down the instinctive templates that will later seek out their completion in the environment.[42]

We now know that we can directly access that same cortical organisation through hypnosis. (The state of deep hypnosis is analogous to that of REM sleep.) Anyone can be put into hypnosis by replicating any part of the pattern by which nature triggers the REM state, such as muscle relaxation, inducing rapid eye movements, (as in the 'focus your eyes on my swinging watch' technique and as used in Eye Movement Desensitisation and Reprocessing, [EMDR]), inducing hemispherical switching to the right neocortex by visualisation (a necessary stage of pre-sleep) or by firing off the brain's orientation response (as when a stage hypnotist suddenly pushes down on his subject's shoulder and gives the instruction "Sleep!"). The orientation response focuses attention and is firing continually during dreaming.[43]

The brain absorbs new ideas and information best when in a receptive, open, uncritical trance state. Once patterns have been absorbed and understood they can be looked at consciously and 'checked out'.

(One of the drawbacks of modern media is that, whenever new ideas are proposed or discoveries announced, they are *immediately* placed in the firing line of confrontational criticism. The absorption stage is bypassed. This is why, for example, debating programmes on television and radio are often un-memorable and unsatisfying.)

In counselling, when we relax people and focus their attention, we create the same hypnotic REM state in which the brain is at its most receptive, able to absorb information uncritically. That is the ideal time in which to offer stories and metaphors to clients' unconscious minds to help them transform their perceptions.

The bigger pattern

Understanding the importance of pattern matching, metaphor and story is fundamental to making teaching more effective and our children more able to develop their full potential in life. Throughout the ages all good teachers have been great storytellers, but only now do we have a physiological under-standing of why it is necessary for them to be so. Research by Professor Ornstein and others shows that, when people are listening to stories, their right hemisphere is very actively engaged in the process. Our left neocortex processes facts and factual information, whereas the right neocortex seems to be involved in creating and revising the 'context' – the bigger pattern – through which facts make sense.[44]

In our technological civilisation we are flooded with factual information from a myriad of sources. But facts on their own don't make us wise. And an excess of facts just raises our stress levels. What makes us wise is fitting facts into a meaningful context, and that is the job of the right neocortex. We, therefore, firmly believe that children need an education that involves history and stories – the patterns that give context and make learning a real experience. It has long been known that child-ren and adults exposed to quality, 'classical' stories (brimming with rich psychological templates) become more flexible in their thought processes, more creative and more intelligent as adults. "Many traditional tales have a surface meaning (perhaps just a socially uplifting one) and a secondary, inner significance, which is rarely glimpsed consciously, but which nevertheless acts powerfully upon our minds. Perhaps above all the tale fulfils the function not of escape but of hope. The suspending of ordinary constraints helps people to reclaim optimism and to fuel the imagination with energy for the attainment of goals: whether moral or material."[45]

The quality of stories is important. Our whole culture is saturated with stories – television soap operas, newspapers, magazines, films, plays and popular songs all contain stories about what's going on in people's lives, fictional or otherwise. Our brains crave stories and metaphors. Once a story starts we have to hear it through; the pattern has to be completed. But the stories our brains receive are not just entertainment. They can have a creative or destructive impact on how we understand life and live our lives.

Some metaphors in our culture come from ideas put forward by scientists and spread through the media and educational institutions to the wider population. These can have a powerful effect – creative or destructive. The view that evolution is the story of 'the survival of the fittest', for example, was used by racial supremacists to justify exploitative colonial policies. This evolutionary theory is only a story, not an actual explanation based on facts.

The 'selfish gene' theory is another attempt to supply a metaphor to explain certain biological processes – one that has taken on a devastating life of its own maintaining the forces of pessimism and hopelessness.[46] What the metaphor says to our culture is that 'life is meaningless'. It can be seen as a cultural form of nocebo.

Whilst few serious scientists question evolution, the overemphasis on the selfish gene idea neglects the cooperative principle found throughout nature for furthering survival. This is evidenced between members of the same species and also in symbiotic relationships between different species and in the huge variety of subtle feedback processes that maintain life in the biosphere.

There is no doubt that stories are powerful. One reason they can have a *positive* effect in influencing behaviour is that, when we give them attention, we actively engage the imaginative side of the mind and go into trance. We open up the part of the brain that can programme in new templates. When children hear a story the pattern is absorbed into their unconscious minds where it will remain available, awaiting opportunities to interpret and unfold more of reality, until the pattern is completed.

Stories contain the wisdom of the species, because knowledge is metaphorically expressed through them and transmitted orally down the generations.

To demonstrate the levels of meaning and the values that can be extracted from such a story we can look at one which adults could easily dismiss as trivial – the story of the Ugly Duckling.

ON A FARM a little bird is raised by a duck but feels itself to be very different from all the other ducklings who keep mocking it for being big and ugly. In due course, the ugly duckling becomes so unhappy it decides to run away, leaves the farm and goes in search of his destiny. But every animal it meets laughs at him for being so ugly and he learns that he can ignore them and not get upset by their stupidity. Eventually he finds a little pond where, despite feeling isolated and lonely, he learns to look after himself and survive through the long, cold winter.

As the months pass by, changes happen within him, although he is unaware of this. One day, in early spring, the pond is still and calm, and in the water he sees the reflection of a line of beautiful swans flying high overhead. He wishes with all his heart that he could somehow be with them. The swans call down saying: "Why don't you join us?" And he said: "How can I, an ugly duckling, fly with beautiful birds like you?" And the swans laugh and say, "But look at your reflection," and the duckling looks at his own reflection in the still pool and realises that he has transformed into a swan. The former ugly duckling is able to join the swans as an equal on their journey.

All children resonate with that story because, at some time, every child feels isolated from their fellows, an outsider who doesn't fit in. There *are* times in life when we feel rejected, when we have to go it alone, when we have got to find the courage to last the course, when our emotional needs are not being properly met. But the template in the story contains more than that. It shows us that, if we approach those times with courage, changes will automatically occur. We can learn from the very deprivations that seem so problematical and, if we persevere and seek out an appropriate environment, our talents and potential can blossom. The story holds out the optimistic prospect that the individual, and perhaps the human species, has somewhere to go; that there is a destiny awaiting us, if we have the courage to seek it, to stretch ourselves and sustain our spirit during troubled times.

Further subtleties include the profound truth, highlighted in this monograph, *that we can only see clearly when we are calm.* If the water on the pond had been disturbed the ugly duckling would not have been able to see what he was like. In other words, children hearing this story are given the template that they need to be in a calm emotional state before they can accurately perceive what they actually are.

At an even deeper level, we might draw out the idea that the emotional brain is like an ugly duckling, but, if we are willing to retrain our responses and cultivate and refine our perceptions, we can become more intelligent and raise ourselves up. It's only, as it were, by escaping the world of the ugly duckling that the true potential of the individual can emerge. And the price that has to be paid is that we may have to go against some of the prevailing orthodoxies within society and tread a lonely path for a while.

The patterns in such a rich story stay with us all, like a protective talisman, for the rest of our lives.

In counselling, when we relax people and focus their attention, we create the same hypnotic REM state in which the brain is at its most receptive, able to absorb information uncritically. That is the ideal time in which to offer stories and metaphors to clients' unconscious minds to help them transform their perceptions.

A summary and an intriguing new thought

The APET theory is at the heart of human givens therapy. The four letters stand for specific processes through which the mind/body system works.

APET

The **A** is for an activating agent: a stimulus from the environment. The **P** is for the pattern-matching part of the mind, which in turn gives rise to an emotion, **E**, which can produce **T**, thoughts.

But these letters also contain a powerful metaphor which enriches the idea. The first three spell 'ape' and that gives us the idea of an ape telling us what to do.

APET

So we have this ancient emotional mind that can order us about, tell us what to do, control us: a mixture of primitive and conditioned responses, greeds and selfish desires which, when roused, can cut us off from the richer and more subtle templates, located in the right and left hemispheres of the higher cortex and the frontal lobes, through which we can experience reality.

On the other hand, if we break up the letters slightly differently, we have 'a pet'.

A PET

A pet is an animal that was originally wild, but its nature has been constrained – domesticated to serve the needs of a master. This is a cooperative relationship. The pet serves the needs of the master and, in return, the master takes care of the needs of the pet. That is the civilising process we humans have to go through – domesticating the emotional brain, the wild, instinctive creature within us.

So, whilst the individual letters symbolise the way the brain processes information, they also describe the essence of the therapeutic process – helping people to 'master' the mind/body system, particularly the more primitive, emotional parts of it, and fulfil our human needs and potential.

In fact, if we accept that nature programmes us with metaphorical patterns, and that we are instinctively seeking to find the completion of those patterns in the environment, perhaps we might have an explanation for what is still a mystery to modern science: the nature of consciousness. Is it, we ask, the spark of recognition when we complete a *significant* pattern match – when the inner template meshes with something outside in the environment and we become aware of it?

Perhaps this matching between the inner and the outer – what creates our world, our universe, and gives meaning to it – *is* consciousness.

And it would follow that, the more subtle the inner templates – the more refined the perceptions – the higher the consciousness available to unfold more of reality.

* * * * *

References

1. Jouvet, M. (1965) Paradoxical sleep – a study of its nature and mechanisms. *Prog Brain Research*, 18, 20–57.

2. Walker, S. *(1983) Animal Thought.* Routledge & Kegan Paul, London, Boston.

3. Gopnik, A., Meltzoff, A and Kuhl, P. (1999) *How Babies Think.* Weidenfeld & Nicolson.

4. Ibid.

5. Zajonc, A. (1995) *Catching the Light.* Oxford University Press.

6. Holland, P. (1999) Just pretending: developing boys' dramatic play in the nursery. *Language Matters*, 2–5.

7. Colapinto, J. (2000) *As Nature Made Him: the boy who was raised as a girl.* Harper Collins.

8. Goleman, D. (1996) *Emotional Intelligence.* Bloomsbury, London.

9. LeDoux, J. E. (1998) *The Emotional Brain.* Weidenfeld & Nicolson.

10. LeDoux, J. E. (1993) Emotional memory systems in the brain. *Behavioural Brain Research*, 58.

11. Libet, B. (1983) Time of conscious intention to act in relation to onset of cerebral activity (readiness-potential); Part 3: The unconscious initiation of a freely voluntary act. *Brain,* 106, 623–42.

12. Danton, W., Antonuccio, D. and DeNelsky, G. (1995) Depression: psychotherapy is the best medicine. *Professional Psychology Research and Practice*, 26, 574.

13. Danton, W., Antonuccio, D. and Rosenthal, Z. (1997) No need to panic. *The Therapist*, 4, 4.

14. Griffin, J. and Tyrrell, I. (1999) *Psychotherapy and the Human Givens.* European Therapy Studies Institute.

15. Ibid.

16. Ellis, A. (1971) *Growth through reason: verbatim cases in rational-emotive therapy.* Wiltshire Books.

17. Beck, A. (1976) *Cognitive Therapy and Emotional Disorders.* New American Library.

18. McMullin, R. E. (1986) *Handbook of Cognitive Therapy Techniques.* W. W. Norton.

19. Johnson, R. (1997) This is not my beautiful wife ... *New Scientist, 22* March, 1997.

20. Robertson, I. (1999) *Mind Sculpture.* Bantam Press. Professor Robertson beautifully described our brains as "vast, trembling webs of neurones ... in flux, continually remoulded, sculpted by the restless energy of the world."

21. Gladwell, M. (2000) *The Tipping Point.* Little, Brown and Company.

22. Griffin, J. and Tyrrell, I. (1998) *Hypnosis and Trance States: a new psychobiological explanation.* European Therapy Studies Institute.

23. Ibid.

24. Battino, R. and South, T. L. (1999) *Ericksonian Approaches*. Crown House Publishing.

25. LeDoux, J. E. (1992) Emotion as memory: anatomical systems underlying indelible neural traces. In S. A. Christensen (ed.) *Handbook of Emotion and Memory*. Erlbaum, Hillsdale, New Jersey.

26. Tehrani, N. (1998) Debriefing: a safe way to defuse emotion? *The Therapist*, 5, 3, 24–29.

27. Ibid.

28. Debunking debriefing. *The New Therapist*, 7, 1, 8.

29. New brief for debriefing. *The Therapist,* 6,1,6.

30. Debunking debriefing. *The New Therapist*, 7, 1, 8.

31. For details of training in this important technique, contact MindFields College of Brief Therapy (Tel: 01323 811440 or website: www.mindfields.org.uk)

32. Griffin, J. and Tyrrell, I. (2001) *The Shackled Brain: How to release locked-in patterns of trauma*. Human Givens Publishing.

33. Melville, J. (1977) *Phobias and Obsessions*. George Allen & Unwin.

34. Rachman, S. and Hodgson, R. (1980) The theory and practice of modifying obsessions. In J. Jenkins, W. Mischel and W. Hartup (eds.) *Obsessions and Compulsions*. Prentice-Hall Inc.

35. Yaryura-Tobias, J. A. and Neziroglu, F. (1997) *Biobehavioural Treatment of Obsessive-Compulsive Spectrum Disorders*. W. W. Norton.

36. Teasdale, J. D. (1988) Cognitive vulnerability to persistent depression. *Cognition and Emotion*, 2, 247–274.

37. Griffin, J. and Tyrrell, I. (2000) *Breaking the Cycle of Depression*. Human Givens Publishing.

38. Dixon, M. and Sweeny, K. (2000) *The Human Effect in Medicine: theory, research and practice*. Radcliffe Medical Press, Abingdon, Oxfordshire.

39. Harrington, A. (ed.) (1997) *The Placebo Effect*. Harvard University Press.

40. Martin, P. (1997) *The Sickening Mind: brain, behaviour, immunity & disease*. Harper Collins.

41. Williams, P. (1998) *Stories that Heal*. (Audiotape) The Therapist Ltd. An account of this case history is given, along with many others, on this audiotape.

42. Griffin, J. (1997) *The Origin of Dreams*. The Therapist Ltd, Sussex.

43. Griffin, J. and Tyrrell, I. (1998) *Hypnosis and Trance States: a new psychobiological explanation*. European Therapy Studies Institute.

44. Ornstein, R. (1993) *The Roots of the Self*. Harper Collins.

45. Shah, I. (1979) *World Tales*. Allen Lane.

46. Behe, M. J. (1996) *Darwin's Black Box*. Simon & Schuster.

About the authors

JOE GRIFFIN is a psychologist with a thriving psychotherapy practice. Over the last decade thousands of health professionals have enjoyed his practical workshops and seminars on effective psychotherapy and counselling. He is widely recognised as one of the most informed and entertaining speakers on the subject having studied with many of the leading figures of the psychotherapy world. He spent 12 years researching why animals and humans evolved to dream. The resulting book which describes the breakthrough he made in this field, *The Origin of Dreams,* offered the first holistic synthesis – a recognition of the interdependence of the biological and the psychological – to explain the origin, function and meaning of dreams. His findings about mental processes have been described by scientific reviewers as, "the key to all psychic states ... an important milestone ... moves our understanding on significantly ... a watershed in our exploration of the evolution of mental processes." He is currently working on a new way of understanding evolutionary processes.

IVAN TYRRELL is a psychotherapist (specialising in brief therapy for depression and anxiety disorders) and a writer with a particular interest in the psychology of perception. He is a founder member of the European Therapy Studies Institute (ETSI) which, in 1992, launched *The Therapist* – the popular multi-disciplinary magazine for all caring professionals. His work for *The Therapist* (now called *Human Givens*) involves him in a continuing programme of writing, interviewing, and investigating the latest developments in psychology, psychotherapy and the study of human behaviour. He lectures at educational and medical institutions throughout the UK. The *British Medical Journal* said of his book, *The Survival Option,* published by Jonathan Cape, "his practical information is reliable", and *The Times* wrote that it contained, "facts, not emotion... should be in every home in the country." Both he and Joe Griffin are members of the group involved with developing the human givens approach to applying knowledge of human psychology and behaviour to psychotherapy, counselling and education.

Organising Idea No. 1

Hypnosis and Trance States

This is the first fully referenced explanation of hypnosis from an evolutionary perspective. *Hypnosis and Trance States: a new psychobiological explanation* offers scientists, researchers, psychologists, psychotherapists, hypnotherapists and the interested lay public, an explanatory 'organising idea' in order to widen and deepen our understanding of the subject. Furthermore, it resolves the controversy of whether hypnosis is an altered state of consciousness or not.

Organising Idea No. 2

Psychotherapy and the Human Givens

There are well over 400 therapies on offer worldwide, with the practitioners of each heavily invested in the principles of their particular approach and often isolated from those whose practice is different. This far-reaching monograph offers an organising idea, drawn from the latest scientific understanding of brain functioning and psychobiology, that enables psychotherapy and counselling to move forward from an agreed basis of what it means to be a healthy human being – using what really works to help when things go wrong.

Organising Idea No. 3

Breaking the Cycle of Depression

Containing a major new insight about the psychobiology of depression derived from the human givens perspective, this monograph quickly demolishes the myths that abound in our society about the subject. It sets out a clear explanation of what depression is and how best to lift it (illustrated by case histories showing how easily this can be done – when you know how).

Organising Idea No. 5

The Shackled Brain: how to release locked-in patterns of trauma

There is a lack of agreement in the medical profession on how best to deal with the often bewildering effects of psychological trauma. Some counselling approaches tend to deepen the trauma rather than remove it. But research shows that we are not all equally susceptible to post traumatic stress disorder (PTSD) – this monograph provides a neurobiological explanation for what happens to the brain of a traumatised person to provoke their disturbing symptoms. It also describes in detail the most effective way to release the locked-in patterns of psychological trauma found in people suffering from PTSD, phobia, panic attacks and obsessive compulsive disorder (OCD).

£4.95 each (plus £1 each p&p) Cheques payable to 'Human Givens Publishing'
From: HG Publishing, The Barn, Church Farm, Chalvington, East Sussex
BN27 3TD. To pay by credit card call: **01323 811662**